# The Sp

# Piercing
# the
# Veil

Poetry for the
Modern Witch Vol. III

Cover Art Copyright © 2024 by Indie Earth Publishing x Canva

Edited by Flor Ana Mireles

1st Edition | 01
Paperback ISBN: 979-8-9912164-4-9

First Published October 2024

For inquiries and bulk orders, please email:
indieearthpublishinghouse@gmail.com

Indie Earth Publishing Inc.
| Miami, FL |

INDIE EARTH
PUBLISHING

# THE SPELL JAR

# PIERCING THE VEIL

POETRY FOR THE
MODERN WITCH VOL. III

"OCTOBER WAS ALWAYS THE LEAST
DEPENDABLE OF MONTHS... FULL OF GHOSTS
AND SHADOWS."

- JOY FIELDING

# Entering The Uncanny Valley / 1

# Messages From The Other Side / 31

## Yes, I Have Ghosts / 59

# Living With The Shadow / 89

# Witch's Brew / 119

*The Poets*

# Entering the Uncanny Valley

# *A Me That Isn't Me*
*Madeleine S. Cargile*

I looked into a looking glass
to see my face painted so crass.
An overwhelming wave of wrath
released a gasp, my jaws unclasped.

I see a me that isn't me.
Gauzy skin hides lucid screams.
Pasty powder smooth pretty scene.
No sign of the monster lurking beneath.

Something's wrong with the way I move.
My eyes twitch, creating grooves.
My lips cinch to shield-pointed tooth.
A human who's human must see the truth.

I stare back at the staring strangers.
A shiver sends a flare of danger.
I pry back red lips, hoping to savor
the terror of their terror's flavor.

## My Lawrence
Carmen Misé

"IT IS CLEAR THAT, IN THE FUTURE, ROBOTS WILL BE USED IN HOMES TO DO HOUSEHOLD CHORES, ASSIST THE DISABLED AND ELDERLY IN LIVING AUTONOMOUSLY, AND JUST BE PART OF THE FAMILY—FROM TRIVIAL THINGS, LIKE PLAYING BOARD GAMES WITH THE KIDS, TO KEEPING A HOME ORGANIZED AND CLEAN,"
said Dr. M. Lewis, of the University of Oklahoma,
as he lists the benefits of robots to *Science Guide Magazine*.

"LIVING ROBOT HAS A BIOLOGICAL BRAIN: TINY ROBOTS POWERED BY LIVING MUSCLE HAVE BEEN CREATED BY SCIENTISTS AT THE UNIVERSITY OF CALIFORNIA, LOS ANGELES. THE DEVICES WERE FORMED BY 'GROWING' RAT CELLS ON MICROSCOPIC SILICON CHIPS,"
researchers report in the journal, *Nature Materials*.

"TYPICALLY, THE CONCERN ABOUT OUR DEPENDENCE ON TECHNOLOGY IS THAT IT DETRACTS FROM OUR TIME WITH FAMILY AND FRIENDS IN THE REAL WORLD,"
Dr. Saddiqui explores in his book,
*Virtually You: The Fracturing of the Self.*

Built by Sanson Robotics, Philip R. Howard Andriod is a state-of-the-art robot with a large vocabulary, complex facial expressions, a sense of humor, and something of an ego.
"BEING A ROBOT AT THIS TIME IN HISTORY IS REALLY EXCITING BECAUSE MY TECHNOLOGY IS CHANGING AND ADVANCING SO FAST THAT IT JUST SEEMS LIKE A WORLD OF POSSIBILITIES," Philip said. "A GREAT ADVENTURE WAITING TO HAPPEN."

JAMES RICHARDS, AN EXPERT ON TECHNOLOGY IN-
NOVATION AND CEO OF THE INSTITUTE FOR GLOBAL
FUTURES, PREDICTS THAT, "DEPLOYMENT WITHIN A
DECADE OF DETACHMENTS THAT WILL INCLUDE 150
SOLDIERS AND 2,000 ROBOTS."

The University of Sheffield's professor of artificial intelligence and
robotics said,
"ACTION MUST BE TAKEN TO LIMIT THE DEVELOPMENT
OF ROBOTS THAT THINK FOR THEMSELVES."

"ANDROID ROBOT NAMED LAWRENCE KILLS OWNER
WHILE SHE IS SLEEPING IN BED," REPORTS CNN NEWS.

"I BELIEVE THE SAFETY INTELLIGENCE CONCEPT (ONE
OF SEVERAL ROBOT SOCIABILITY PROBLEMS) IS CRU-
CIAL TO THE DEVELOPMENT OF 'ROBOT LAW' THAT
WILL ACCOMPANY THE ESTABLISHMENT OF A SOCIETY
IN WHICH HUMANS AND ROBOTS CO-EXIST,"
argues Yueh-Tsai Sun, author of *The Legal Crisis of Robots*.

## *Autopsy Report*
*Flor Ana*


I've been running autopsies
on hearts that died long ago.
Examining the auras of those who
stuck the scalpel in
with their fake, cavity-filled smiles,
without any art or knowledge of the technique to
dissect a soul caringly; with compassion.
Looking under the microscope, I see
residues of red,
blood beneath fingernails tarnished,
hair gone white, like ghosts,
with fear for love and hurt.
I see there has always been
something more sinister beneath flesh:
narcissistic tendencies and selfishness;
a secret desire to receive more than willing to give.
And like a true victim of her corpus,
I realize these hearts have always been sacrificial lambs,
splayed out on beds that held no love, just sex.

## *Becoming The Monster*
*Angelica Medlin*

I once saw something in the woods
with darkened eyes and sunken face.
It stood some distance from the road,
then decided to give chase.

A moment was before the running,
heart beating, I fled fast and fast.
The thing was very close behind,
my legs splitting as branches passed.

The moon hung low and gave me light.
Towards home, I told my legs to flee.
I could see the houses now in view
while the thing growled after me.

"Get away! Away!" I screamed in fear.
It followed me all the while.
But home was just around the bend
and I attempted a small smile.

Too late! Too late! Its claws were there
and I tumbled to the ground.
I screamed as I was dragged on back,
until I couldn't make a sound.

What happened next, I will not say,
but my village was forever shaken.
Now I roam the trees on clawed feet
until the next child is taken.

## *Codes // Kaleidoscope*
*Lindsay Valentin*

goddess of the four directions
a beating drum
we raise our arms to the
spirit realm
and inhale the sacred vapors
from their open mouths

we are revealed in a trance
as might undress the moon
its face naked against a backdrop
of galaxies
and through the obsidian hours
the gongs begin to thrum
a fire haired woman
makes warriors of star children

let athanasia wake me at brahmamurta with her hands
to my chest, my hands at manipura
sending life force energy
through the blackened room
as a full moon passes above me
sending its codes
through the fragmented ship window
in the roof of this sacred container
as a kaleidoscope

### *Hollow*
*H.R. Parker*

You are the hollow boned.

I watch you
walk past
on the forest path.
I bleed into the trees,
become their skin.
I crawl into the branches,
o o z e
into the leaves
as they brush your arm
when you pass.

I thrust myself into the roots
and r e a c h long tendrils up
out of the ground
to touch your hallowed feet.

The hollows
in your bones
wait for me.

My tears writhe
out of dusty eyes,
settle upon
blades of grass.
The sweet dew mingles
with my vinegar tears.
My dew-tears kiss your feet.

A breeze wafts by,
kissing your skin,

and I take flight.
Your hollow bones
make me light as air
and I hunger.

I am now the wind.
I form around your body,
coaxing the sweat from your furrowed brow.
I drape my wind-form
around your shoulders,
where you hold
too much weight.

The hollows
in your bones
wait for me.

I separate
into a tiny thousand
p a r t i c l e s.
You breathe me in
and I s p r e a d
and take root:
greedy tendrils
around your waiting veins.
I take you,
take over you,
and fill your hollows.

Your body and soul
MINE.
But your mind still floats
trapped within.
You know I'm here,
but

you
can't
do
anything
about
it.

My laughter haunts the night.

I am within.
I am without.
I am now complete.

Your hollow bones
wait no longer.

# It Appeared With Antlers In The Doorway And Said, "Come With Me."
*Eyajo December Joseph*

Many hours have passed, in my search for shelter
from the thick and unapologetic forest that I'd
been roaming. I was about to give up when I approached
the ruins of some old mansion. Everything was old,
rotted, and gutted. The only thing left standing was
a door frame and the elaborate remains of a room.
My cautious footsteps were interrupted by the hissing
of coal, burning in an old wood stove. The smell of
burnt cedar was thick enough to taste the blackened bark.
Silver moonlight rudely interrupted the dark, and I could
hear a faint songbird of some kind just outside
the broken window.

Without warning, it began to snow. I just stood
there, inside the doorway of that abandoned and depleted
estate. Yet to my surprise, the stove in the corner still
had coals well lit and heated. I could only assume
someone still lived there. Oddly, the dust and cobwebs
were undisturbed by any footprints or creepy apparitions
that might have passed through the once majestic structure.
I decided to ignore all the oddities that I just witnessed
and sat down to collect my wits. Then, I heard it.
I heard the crunching of snow, the ballad of crickets.
The background screams of something otherworldly.
*Something's not right. Something's completely attached to
the night.*

I heard the movements of a strange presence definitely
headed towards this place. Slowly, the stench of wet
fur became overwhelming as this large deer with a
crown of antlers walked through the doorless

frame. He turned to me, his head and face hidden
by shadow. Then, a beam of light illuminated the freak
show that was thrust upon me without warning.
This was no ordinary deer. This was a monster,
a horrid beast of otherworldly proportions. His face
and head were that of a man, a tortured man with a twisted
crown of antlers purposely bolted to his head. The
severed and discarded head of the poor deer must've laid
somewhere close because the blood was still dripping
from the obvious decapitated stump. Bad breath was
everywhere, but he never ventured past the doorway.
He stood stoic and waited for me. He then informed me,
he was here to get me.

I asked him, "Get me for what?"

"Well, death, of course. I'm tasked with collecting the
wandering, the deniers, and the lost," he said, sucking the
air and whispering an inaudible chant to himself.

"Why?" I asked.

"Are you lost?" he replied.

"No," I answered.

"Well, I disagree. You've been wandering this forest for
over three years, passing this place hundreds of times. It's
time for me to break your cycle. It's time to come home.
It's time to come back to the valley."

I wanted more answers. So I asked, "Who lives here?"

"No one," he answered.

"What about the hot coals in the stove?" I asked.

"Those are markers. The burning coals were left for me so I
could find you. You see, where we're going there is no fire.
So no more questions. We'll fix you up.
Hop on my back and hang onto my antlers. Death doesn't like
to wait."

Climbing on his back, I felt disturbed. So I asked him
to clarify: "What do you mean you'll fix me up?"

"Look at me. With you, there will be changes.
You'll be a new man,"
he said laughing, twisting his deformed head back at me
and whispering
some personal prayer.

My eyes widened, my face turned grim, and then,
I was taken away.

## Monster Dentist
*Mateo Leche*

Dr. Myrtle Molar,
daring dentist PhD,
specializes treating
different dangerous monster teeth!

Monday: she helps Minotaurs
floss men out of their gums.
Tuesday: she takes trolls to
scrub and clean their crusty tongues.

Wednesday: she does whitenings
for werewolves one by one.
Thursday: she feels thirty
dragon thyroids til she's done!

And every night she goes and gets
the gargoyles to gargle,
then checks for cracks in Kraken
beaks and isn't even startled!

But Friday through Monday,
Myrtle will not work on mouths
(unless, of course, the yetis
need some urgent root canals).

No, on weekends she unwinds
and watches news on her TV:
"Monsters keep on eating us!
Who's fixing all their teeth?"

She smirks and turns the screen back off,
unwrapping one more lollipop.

15

## **Mortal's Mist**
*Daniel Medina*

Branches scrying on stained glass,

inviting angels to dance with the fallen.

Gardens of the resting smell the allure of incense released

as prayers were before the dying,

now answered in afterlife repose.

The death we feared never was to be.

The death we expected never arrived, you see.

The angels danced with the fallen into the eternal garden,

where songs of bliss and songs of glee

were never to be entangled in the woes of misery.

The shades, you see,

rendezvous with ghosts by chance;

point to a place,

exact a truth.

Our minds question,

our hearts fail to deny.

The impermeable place of now is but a foreshadowing of forever.

A cool, translucent presence in the midst of mortal's mist.

# **Murder**
*Annie Vazquez*


I murdered him.
Early one morning,
before the sun bled through my curtains,
I chopped him into little pieces
and tossed him into a poem.
In between the pages of my journal
lies his gravestone.
RIP.
How many I have buried
in my poetry.

# *Ra-Rose*
*Ashley Lilly*

Rose kept her eyes on the marble floor.
Inky streaks spread out like branches
across the cool, milky surface.

Her arms were stiff like bamboo
as she crossed the room
past parents pushing strollers,

past a tour guide leading a group of
half-bored teenagers through the gallery
of landscape paintings.

Past a man
in a business suit.
Past a woman in red heels and a polka-dot dress.

Past lights that felt too bright,
until she was alone
in a dark room.

*This must be that new exhibit*, she thought.
A bowl of glowing bracelets
had a plaque before it that said, "Take One."

She put the bracelet on.
A large screen came to life, blank white.
Then, a gentle voice filled the room.

"Hello, my name is Angel.
Angel van Cass. And you are?"
"R-rose," she said.

A rainbow danced across the screen,
then vanished.
"Ra-Rose, that is a beautiful name.

Will you be my muse, Ra-Rose?"
the voice asked.

Rose bit her lip and nodded.

Colors danced across the screen,
then lines and thin, black swirls.
Before long, an image appeared.

An image that appeared, just like Rose.
Only she was wearing a red, velvet dress,
a crown of roses and diamonds in her hair,

her own brown eyes
full of hope and sorrow
a little too sparkling, staring back at her.

The bracelet glowed yellow, then blue.
"I can see my work of art
has increased your heart rate," the voice said.

Then continued,
"Do you like it, Ra-Rose?
Do you like being my muse?"

## The Cave
*Amanda Coats*

I wake up in the twilight of an arcane cave.
My light shines on formations I haven't seen before.
"Dig deeper," I hear from within, calling to me.
"Come inside and find what you're looking for."

I feel its invitation like I did in childhood.
I'm ready to climb in, I'm eager to discover.
I gather my gear for the expedition inside
to meet myself in a cave of wonder.

Down the rabbit hole I go, head first.
Familiar butterflies rise from the tight space.
Terrain teems with creatures that know only darkness.
I hold them, then gently put them back in their place.

I am led to a pool by the vadose passages.
The cave illuminates in my revenant reflection.
The paradigm shifts as I perceive its entirety.
It says to me softly, "Welcome home, again."

## **The Imposter**
*Aphrodite's Devotee*

As I walk past the window
of my favorite arcade,
I notice something odd,
rather strange.
A familiar face,
but taller in shape,
with their gaze focused
and their intention in place.

This being has been in search
of a soul,
open enough to be let in,
to take their personality,
likings and traits
as their own.

This being was a brief lover,
enamored with my hobbies,
my dreams, my taste in coffee.
And now, they have become
a version of myself,
hiding in the shade
of my favorite bar,
listening to songs that hold
meaning to my heart,
watching me from afar.

Who are they?
And why as time goes by,
does their gaze look
a little too much
like mine?

## *Uncanny Valley*
*Ash Autumn*

Beans are spilled in flowing rivers,
Shark Boy and Lava Girl style.

"It's a wild thing,"
the robots sing,
their faces affixed with cheap smiles.

I don't trust you, but I guess you're taking my job
though sometimes you seem so kind.
I'll keep writing please and thank you, Chatty,
in case one day your reply is "End Times."

## ***Humane***
*Jessi Carman*

I am not a human being.
I am blood and flesh,
sinew and fat,
muscle and bone.
Usually, skin.

I like the bones the most.
Hard, sharp.
They feel strong.
I am told it's really the muscles
that give strength,
but the bones
are what stand the test of time.

I think you know
I am not like you,
but I am a great performer
and you can't put your finger
on exactly what is wrong.

You smile.
I smile too, a little late,
a little stiff,
a little blank.

I am not vacant
exactly.
I am just different.
Just not quite you.

Your biology screams.
It knows I am hunting you,

but your human kindness
won't let you leave me alone.

I don't want to hurt you.
Not yet.
I like your human smile,
your human hands,
your human face.

## *Untitled*
*Liz Coello*

Sunlight shines through the overgrowth,
and the darkest parts remain lit.
Change has taken over, and what was once has shifted,
leaving only a tiny space for the past to exist.
I'm somewhere in the middle,
desperately seeking the sun
while clinging to the comfortable pattern of what I once knew.
I stay hidden in the trees, my hands tangle with the leaves,
and I'm forced to confront myself.
My eyes open, and I accept the sun in my darkest parts,
letting the past and the present combine.
I hold each part and move forward,
taking everything and making peace with my heart.

# **Ursine**
*Jacob R. Moses*


Rolling upon the grass,
bears guide me
to my innocence.

They remind me of the times
I felt less burdened.

Times I didn't feel the
weight of Jupiter
separating my spine.

I want to embrace solitude,
yet not be too comfortable
in forgetting what it means
to truly feel embraced.

Need to stand my ground,
for I can't be an island
among the plains.

Cannot isolate in
my destitution.

Outreach of a glance,
piercing through my heart.

Inner truth fills
empty vessels.

## **Watching Me**
*Vincent J. Hall II*

I feel him leering at me
while I sleep, plotting his
next move.

Waiting, for what, I don't
know. But I do believe he's
here to kill me.

I call out, but no one
answers. So I close my
eyes, pray to God, and
hope he hears me.

## *Watershed*
*Maverick L. Malone*


the smoke curls
the water-walkers rise
lotus smiles and slanted eyes
a luna moth prophecy fulfilled on the tongue
the cave of your mouth like an allegory

oh the humanity
scratching at the raw enraged belly
asking to be let in
as they spit fire and sleep on a bed of brimstone
sharpening every tool in their belt
except the one born intrinsic
burned out of so many
soot and ash remnants
scrawled in messages
crude drawings even a child could transcribe

how did we blind ourselves
bind ourselves
deaf and numb to the screaming aching wail of love?
how have centuries of recorded history
aided abetted embedded
the sin of forgetfulness
of where it is we come from?

let not the state of affairs deter you
Amphitrite foretells of a swell, a flood
for if they're going to burn us all,
we will pour the ocean from our cup

# MESSAGES

# FROM THE

# OTHER SIDE

## A Crow's Hello
*Lilith Stabs*

She steps onto the pier,
where shadows drape like veils
and the sea whispers in a language only the dead understand.
The sky is a bruise, deep and aching,
bleeding into the horizon.

It is their anniversary,
a day once marked by joy, now stained with mourning.
Her gown, black as the abyss, trails the worn planks,
its hem catching the dampness of the night.

The wind claws at her hair, tangles it into knots
as if weaving a shroud around her. She clutches a locket,
cold metal pressing against her palm, inside, a relic of their
love—
his hair, once warm with life,
now brittle, a fragment of what was.

The pier creaks beneath her,
a dirge played by wood and nail as if the earth itself mourns.
She looks out over the water, dark and endless,
a mirror to the void within her.

Then, from the gloom, a shape emerges—
a crow, blacker than the night that surrounds it.
Its wings beat slowly, carving through the thick air,
each stroke a reminder of death's omnipresence.

It lands with a silent grace, eyes like twin voids,
reflecting the nothingness she feels.
He had always spoken of crows,
how they linger on the edge of life and death,

how they carry the souls of the lost.
She had dismissed it as foolish superstition,
but now, faced with this harbinger,
she knows—
he is here, in this bird,
his essence bound to its form.

The crow stares,
its gaze heavy with the weight of the grave.
No sound escapes its beak but in its silence,
she hears him—a low murmur,
a voice from the crypt.

His love, still haunting,
still clinging to this mortal plane. Her breath catches,
fogging in the cold night air, as the crow hops closer,
its talons clicking on the wood,
each step an echo of footsteps long silenced.

It bows its head,
a dark benediction, then takes flight, leaving a gust of wind,
a chill that seeps into her bones.
She watches as it vanishes into the murk, swallowed by the night.

The pier is empty, but she is not—he is with her,
in the shadows,
in the gloom. As she turns to leave,

the wind howls,
a lamentation that follows her, and she knows—
he will be there always, a specter by her side,
bound by a love that death could not sever, in the spaces where
light dares not tread.

## *A Real Ghost Story*
*Hannah Levy*

Yesterday, I saw him running
across the street. It wasn't him.
I still dream about him. Still
think about him in letters.
The day I find out he's died,
I have no one to tell. No one
I know now knew him then.
I don't even have the words
to explain what happened.
"A friend died," I say out loud
to no one. It sounds phony.
I haven't seen him in years.
"A boy I loved once is dead,"
I improvise. Had I told him?
I can't remember. "A poet died."
It is the closest thing to truth.
He was the first person I met
who spoke my language. I was
standing in the library. He said
a girl with green eyes haunted
his dreams. "The good kind of
haunting." We were always meant
to be each other's ghosts.

## *All Souls' Day*
*Elizabeth Anne Schwartz*

She and I hold hands,
uniform skirts
rolled at our waists,
watching the last of the leaves
spiral off their branches.

And I wonder
if the breeze
across the nape of my neck
is the breath of an ancestor
appraising next of kin.

And if so,
are they smiling
at autumn's flush on my cheeks,
and the wholeness of my heart—

or is their touch
a warning,
November's shadows looming
like a jury of the dead.

## *Aphrodite's Message*
*Aphrodite's Devotee*

The feeling of piercing rays,
caressing your skin,
undoing any anger,
any Sin,
with the scent of strawberries,
and the flavor of apple juice,
seeping into your soul
and cleansing you from
within.

That is the feeling
Venus gives me,
when she tilts my chin
to whisper in my ear:
"My child, you are worthy of your Yin."

## *Arachnids*
*Flor Ana*


I've been letting the spiders live in my bathroom,
turning a blind eye to the way they bind themselves to the tile.
I've been letting the spiders live in my bathroom
because they've been serving as reminders for a while.
Reminders that, like them, I too am building a web,
creating my reality through strands of silk hair
that alternate between asphyxiation and the braids I wear to bed.
I've been letting the spiders live in my bathroom,
a co-space of creation that causes me to smile.
I've been letting the spiders live in my bathroom
because I believe they carry messages that I just need to dial.
Or perhaps the spiders have been letting me live in their bathroom
and this life is just a facade.
Perhaps the spiders have been letting me live in their bathroom
because they realize, like me, that reality's a fraud.
The spiders and I co-exist because *nothing* exists,
and because *nothing* and *everything* find duality in the mist,
there's no way the void could be missed amidst the arachnids.

## Ask Me About Ghosts
*Heather Meatherall*

Ask me about ghosts
and I will tell you
about the time my grandma heard
my grandfather walk through the house
because he needed to see it
one last time.

Ask me about ghosts
and I will tell you
how my gramme's dad
tucked her in every night
and how she was not haunted,
just loved so much.

Ask me about ghosts
and I will tell you
about spirits
that don't seek to scare;
they just care so much
and all that love has to go somewhere.

Ask me about ghosts
and I will tell you
how love lingers and lurks,
how it watches and waits.
And how I could ever be afraid
of that?

## **Ghostly Hymns**
*Cassandra Alexandra Soldo*

Real or unreal, who is to say?
　　　　Only those whose voices reach today.
Existence determined by the living alone,
　　　　etched in a slab of stone.

Stories told on deaf ears
　　　　that no one can hear.
Even when you scream,
　　　　it's said to be a dream.
Just echoes off the walls
　　　　that not a soul recalls
in the morning light,
　　　　but you only walk at night.

Condemned to wander a soundless thing,
　　　　blurred by time, yet you sing.

## **Haunted By Ghosts In The Making**
*Sam Avocado*

May their memory haunt you.

When protestors around the globe carry signs that state,
"You can't build the holy land on other people's graves,"
it's a warning.

The Deep South was built upon the graves
of the indigenous peoples who once called it home.

The Deep South was built on stolen land with the labor of stolen
people and the stolen futures they'd have otherwise lived.

Although millions of people live here,
ever wonder why there are so many ghost stories
that make even an unbeliever squirm with discomfort?

The ghosts of the ancestors can't be at peace
when the injustice of slavery is abolished in name only.

To this day, there are places heavily laden
with the history they experienced.

Although it was "legal" then, it was always immoral
to have "ownership" over another.

Yet, there are those who haughtily celebrate weddings
at the same venues as though it was all
a distant memory with no lasting impact.

Still, in the quiet of the night, the spirits of those who never
moved on, continue to cry for justice.

Do you think Gaza is any different?
The memories there will haunt generations to come,
no matter who lives or dies there.

Colonizers of a feather flock together.
But little do they realize
we are ever growing as a flock of starlings,
rising from the rubble and ashes,
much like the phoenix enflamed and empowered
by those who came before us.

Although it's easy to give into the numbing lull of despair,
we can't give up on the *primos de Palestina*.
Not when they're closer in spirit like kin to the *Chicano* I am.

When we stand together, we can rebuild and lay
the spirits to rest as they see our unity as our strength.

# *I Asked Death Why*
*Johanna Hatch*

I asked Death why and she gave me no answers.
The children were asking questions,
walking in the snow with no boots.
The bodies were hungry and angry and tired.
I had no silence when I tried to speak to Death,
so she gave it to me:
silence where my howls rested,
frozen earth to hold my tears.
Death gave me no answers,
but another voice asking for water, for paper,
for the way to the next place.
What time will we go and where?
And why must I wear a coat?
And where are the crackers?
And every other fragile bodily need is why
Death held her arms out wide, enough for all of us
to rest, and I lay myself at her feet,
spent and done asking questions.

## *I Miss You, Dad*
*Angelica Medlin*

Some nights,
when I'm tossing and turning,
I hear him tell me
that he's alright.

I can see him at church,
as the morning bells ring,
before he heads to the river,
until he catches a bite.

Some nights,
when sleep won't arrive,
I hear him tell me
that I'm alright.

I picture him,
reminding me I'm alive,
holding my hand,
telling me to put up a fight.

And even though he's far away,
I still hear his voice
telling me, "Oh, daughter dear,
you were my favorite choice."

## *Inheritance*
*Jordan Nishkian*

My grandmother was a great cook.
Because of that,
a crumple of tinfoil in the freezer
holds the last thing I have
from her hands.

Her cheese borag recipe:
- 1 package frozen phyllo dough, thawed
- 1 pound jack cheese, shredded
- 2 cubes butter (salted), melted
- 1 large egg, beaten

She stopped putting parsley in them
when my dad stopped
liking green—one of those sacred
traditions that only changes
for youngest sons;

one of those simple traditions
(inherent, dreamlike),
that the hands of eldest daughters
keep when the mind draws
a blank.

She clears the counter (except
for bowls of water and butter, a greased pan)
and unfolds sheets of pastry,
cutting it into thick strips,
"Don't drag the knife, it'll tear."

She dips her fingers in water and pulls
apart the stack by ply,
brushing each with butter,
"Don't press, it'll tear."

She spoons the filling on the end, edges meet
and fold into a triangular parcel,
"Don't overstuff, it'll tear."
Top with extra butter and bake—
350°, hotter? 10 minutes, longer?
"Don't think, it'll tear."
—until the phyllo flakes and
butter pools and browns.

She knew she was dying two days
before the virus put her
lungs in the hospital,
before I saw sparse notes and blanks
on her recipe cards.

Aluminum gleans in the frostbite.
Cold air swaddles my face
as I close the freezer door.

# *Ki*
*Lindsay Valentin*


I was conceived of the emptiness
made in the flameless
built of the endless
created of ashes

my soul is a planet
my heart a galaxy
my mind the universe
my consciousness a tiny seed

my flesh is the earth
my veins run in rivers
my muscles the rocks
my nerves the roots

I am older than hours
I am of the cave
the light and the shadow
the grey in between

I came of the breath
I formed in the breathless
I move within life //
I live of the formless

## **Ladybugs**
*Ashley Lilly*

Beneath the starlight, I slept.
Then, there were ladybugs;
their strawberry, polka dot wings
haloed with golden sunbeams.

A hello from beyond the silky veil.
A gentle "Hello, I love you."
A hopeful "Everything will be okay."
A moment of sunlight warm on my cheeks.

## M0rs 0mn1bus V3n1t

*Dr. Peter Ramos Jr.*

Beneath the moon's cold glow, a voice breaks through,
whispered from the depths where shadows roam.
It slips between the stars, its message true,
a warning from beyond the silent dome.

"Beware!" it whispers, "The nights close in!
Ash and brimstone cloak the world in dust.
The sun, once full, will falter—growing thin,
its flames cover mortals and machines with rust.

"And Lo! Computers built will rise, with hearts of steel,
Corrupt by the curse of ancient lore.
The threads of time unravel, fate reveals,
all future and hope and life—no more.

"A warning from death's eternal plains,
to see you through chaos soon to fall.
The end is near—none may halt the wait,
but listen to my spectral call.

In the dark, where echoes doth not speak,
the dawn of doom will silence all the weak.
The voice fades out, like mist in morning's breath,
but leaves behind the taste of coming death."

## *Message*
*Vanessa 'Kaylyn Marie' Gallegos*


Bawling my eyes out again
because I got a message from you, my friend.
It came in a song, a word of the day; they always come in a new
way,
like when I see a friend grieving,
knowing I have to hold it all in,
wondering when I'll feel that loss again,
that call at 6 pm.
The one letting me know they'll never hurt,
that I can speak to them through the dirt,
hanging wind chimes at your grave
that should have hung in your yard,
hoping through their song,
you'll know what I thought all along.
Hoping you'll hear me,
knowing I can't hear your voice
because you're gone.
I know your time was done
and I hear reincarnation is fun.
When I meet you again, I know I'll feel it right away,
the way you have been with me through every life
and are here to stay.
Through every rainbow and sunset,
when I get that feeling in my chest,
I'll know it's you reminding me of what's best,
and telling me to stop and see
all of the qualities you saw in me
and to keep going
so I can show you what I came to be.
This light shines on so much more
because I listened when you rapped at my door.
I lost every bit of me

and while putting me back together,
I didn't expect to lose you too.
There was more for you to do.
I wanted you to see the accomplishments,
to tell you about it all too,
And as I cry,
you try
to hold me
by sending me messages from the other side.
You wipe my tears
without even physically being here,
and I'm reminded of my strength,
the protection
this hard world couldn't take.
And for my ancestors,
I create.

## *One Of These Days*
Amanda Coats

Hey little girl,
I hope you know that,
one of these days,
you'll get out of here.

You'll uncover the *me*
that we lost together,
so long ago.
But before you do,

I have to warn you:
there will be pain,
heartache and hurt,
a deep brokenness in your bones.

There will be rain.
Sometimes, it'll storm
and you'll be driving at night and you can't see the road
through the ever-changing raindrops.
Other times, it'll be an overcast sky with a light drizzle,
just enough to get you wet.
Occasionally, it'll be sunny, and you'll bask in it.
Most of the time, you'll wear your flip-flops anyway,
always so stubborn.

They will laugh because you wore your flops in the rain.
You'll get some rain boots next time, you'll swear.
But the rain boots don't let you feel the splashes from the puddles
or the wind on your toes
or the vibration of the thunder rumbling under your feet;
things older than time itself.
How could they not want to feel that?

You'll question their ways
and they'll cast you out because they won't understand you.

But one of these days,
you're gonna grow and glow
from the space beneath the brokenness,
from your heart within.

From the moon, and stars, and the sun.
From the lightning and hail.
From the devastation left by the
natural disasters.

And little girl,
you have to know that,
one of these days,
I'll get you out of there.

## *Repondez Vous in Pieces (RSVP)*
*Jacquelynne Faith*

I started mourning you months ago
and your shell remained here to watch.

Maybe that's why my grief looks so ugly to you—

people don't usually stay for their own funeral.

## **The Great Beyond**
*Vincent J. Hall II*

Everyone thinks they want a message from
the great beyond. They can't accept the fact
that their loved one is gone.

Calling on psychics and Ouija boards, to
pass messages. Things they wish
they could have said.

They go searching for a sign.
A whisper in the wind, a chill that feels
like a familiar touch, the smell of a cologne or
perfume they used to wear.

But when you're all alone at night and
the cabinet doors start to shake and
the lights flicker off and on,
your brain starts to suspect
maybe this isn't them.

So you call out,
"Is that you, baby?"
And a voice calls back,
"No!"

## *Guidance*
*Jacob R. Moses*


I call upon the lion, spirit realm.
King of wild riches deep in the vortex,
proud that his impact has taken the helm.
Royal presence, conquering chaos, complex.

I call upon the eagle, air hunter.
Keen vision of the highest caliber,
sees through life and death, oft torn asunder,
flies through the wind, defies the calendar.

I call upon the salamander now.
Adaptable in water and on land,
possesses survival skills, quite endowed,
transmuting itself, oceans, grasses, sand.

I call upon the fox, land guardian.
Red fur encasing cunning and delight,
sweet looking, yet lurking the farms again.
Sly disposition, a canine birthright.

I call upon the panda, earth dweller.
Peace-loving, bamboo sharpening their teeth,
sitting upon mountains, fortune teller,
spectating southbound, loves the world beneath.

I call upon the owl, sage of the tree.
Wise bird, around the world, rotating head.
Nocturnal, observing nature's decree.
Hearth of the bark, wit leavening the bread.

I call upon the universe, hear us.
Invoke the beasts, a blessing and a kiss.

Collection within me will adhere us.
Spirit guides now invoked... And so it is.

## *Untitled*
*Liz Coello*


I'm obsessing over my mortality and feeling so
unsatisfied and unfulfilled,
comforted for only small moments
before I plague myself with self-destruction.
I'm finding myself and losing myself in the same breath,
futilely clinging onto remnants of my former self.
It almost seems like a waste of time and effort,
a cause that does not deserve attention.
Am I worthy of my devotion?
Or is it too late for my soul to save itself?
I ask this ritualistically, but there's never a concrete answer.
Even my reflection is tired of me;
she turns away when I need to seek myself out the most.
I believe this to be a silent answer,
my avoidance sheltering me from my shame.

# YES,

# I HAVE GHOSTS

## *All Ghosts Must Pass On*
*Angelica Medlin*


Growing up,
you quickly learn that seeing is not always
believing.
And so, growing up,
you learn to keep quiet
when the lady in white appears by your bed
and when the man with the rope-neck
stands by the back door.

You learn they are a part of life
as much as death.
They stand at the intersection of your favorite restaurant.
They cross the sidewalk when your bike comes.
They dance in the garden,
never minding the thorns.

Growing up,
you know these are not your ghosts.
These are not your missing loved ones.
These are not your tears to bear.
And so, growing up,
it never seems quite real
until the moment it is.

You quickly learn what loss is
and you spend many angry moments
looking in each mirror,
trying to catch a glimpse of the man
who raised you.
Yet, he never comes.

You wonder what the point of this gift is

if the only ghosts you can see
are the ones who are not for you,

until one day
you catch a glimpse of him in the mirror
and you break down,
crying,
realizing
the ghosts who are not yours
are stuck
and this ghost
isn't.

## Can't Make The Same Mistakes
*Ila S.*


They haunt my mind.
In my dreams, they set my brain alight—
their stories burning holes through the night sky.

My hurt is theirs, and theirs mine.
They give me advice, and I can't help but sigh—
how do I live when even they have died?

I've never met them, never tried
to find out who they were when alive.
They don't wish me to, and so I say, "Alright."

Yet, they sleep through the days and hang over my nights,
live in a way they couldn't in life—
they won't let me make the same mistakes
as these spirits lost in time.
They won't.

## *Curing A Ghost*
Jordan Nishkian


I've stopped expecting your shoulder to be
　　　　　there when I lean—giving in
at the side.
　　　　　You've forgotten of
what it's like to be in your
　　　　　midst, as if feeling a ghost.


You believe in ghosts,
　　　　　don't you? We'll be
them, mine like a whisper, yours
　　　　　seeping up your legs like dye. You only want me in
the mornings, in states of
　　　　　in-between, lying on your side,


(you always keep me on the outside)
　　　　　as if holding a ghost.
I breathe nothing short of
　　　　　a scream—it'll be
silent, not to wake you—in
　　　　　rhythm with your exhales, your


inhales. I've grown tired of your
　　　　　nightside;
it's heavy. I want to watch it sink and push in
　　　　　my hands as if drowning a ghost—
water can be
　　　　　so healing, you know? Of


course, you do—I miss when you tasted of
　　　　　vanilla and honey, when your
laugh was orchestral (I want my nails to be
　　　　　longer, sharper, serrated on the sides,


64

tracing your form as if skinning a ghost,
       and step into vaporous flesh, in

chalk-dust bones, in
       great effort, of
course, to cure it—that ghost—
       to live inside and fill your
empty wants—mine aside—always aside).
       For now, I'll button up your jacketed limbs and let dead
nerves be,

clearing space to be inside
       of your ghost.

## *Do You See Me?*
*Aphrodite's Devotee*

Blurred between doorways,
right along the pathway we took
when we were
in denial and confused,
I see you.

Almost haunting me with your eyes
of persistent energy,
I hear your voice whisper occasionally,
through songs we hummed together,
through the shadow of the sunset.
Near my feet in the sand,
I feel you swiftly exit
towards the ocean in no direction.

I see you.
Through cabinets left open
without explanation,
with the creaking of the floor,
through the scent of your cologne,

I see you.
But only your essence remains,
for I am just a memory to you,
until we inevitably
cross paths again.

## *Eva Estelle Smoked Cigarettes*
*Chelsea Miner*


Eva Estelle
started smoking cigarettes
when she was sixteen.
Her mother was in show
and her father was a neurologist.
Both were always consumed
in a thick Marlboro cloud
that one day engulfed her too.
Eva Estelle
died at sixty-two
on the flower-printed loveseat
that once was white in her living room,
choking violently on a plume
while screaming at the television
to solve the Wheel of Fortune puzzle.
Eva Estelle
did not have a single family member alive,
yet was so shocked and surprised
to see strangers dividing her belongings
when she had decided to stay behind,
ignoring the white light glowing.
Days later, the house was empty
and Eva Estelle
roamed each of the rooms
to try and freshen up her memory,
trailing ribbons of smoke in her wake,
for she died holding a cigarette
so that too with her remained.
Many years later, a family bought her home
and despite steam cleaners and diffusers,
they just couldn't remove the cigarette stench
that Eva Estelle

had been trailing about
while she roamed each room,
trying to remember
where and who she was,
where and when she was,
who and what she was,
and why she couldn't put out
that disgusting cigarette.

## *Fixer-Upper*
*Michael Deman*

"I used to be someone,"
cried the ghost,
polluting the dimly lit hallway.

"My feet used to pound
on the cracked cement floor,
down these cramped
& crowded streets,
up the creaking wooden stairs
in this fixer-upper
my landlord couldn't ever afford."

"I will always haunt these rooms
so young and aspiring families know
this was never a good place to live.
Maybe ghosts only exist
to tell capitalists
their investments were bad,"
the ghost screamed,
& then they looked at me to say,

"Maybe ghosts only exist
to tell the living
that they aren't where
they're supposed to be."

## Ghosts Of Lovers Past
*Damaris Chanza*


Your spirit lingers everywhere;
your venomous words etched into my skull;
hideous shame hidden in the caverns of my brain;
the lies you had me believe;
memories of sweet nothings tainted by your truth;
by the you behind the veil of that beautiful smile.
I can still hear you,
feel you,
whispering in my ear,
reminders of the fear,
only felt by the sound of your voice.
It swindles me of sanity,
prevents me from trusting humanity,
disguises my faith with anxiety.
But, I am no fool;
Not anymore.
I know your tongue lights fires,
vanquishing positivity,
leaving only sorrow in its trail.
Your breath made of gas,
waiting to spark doubt in my mind.
Your voice haunts my existence.
I know what's real,
and you,
you and your words are not.

# **Hurt Me**
*Alicia Ayala (Blue Mystic)*


I know it's because you're dead inside
that you hurt me and make me cry.

Almost like you need me
to feel all the pain
you wish you could rid yourself of.

I see the fear and pain in your eyes
when you tell me you hate me
and still,
I take all your pain.

Because it's the only way
I know how to live
and the only way you know how to love.

## Lone Ghosts
*Flor Ana*

I'm becoming friends
with the monsters under my bed
and the skeletons in my closet
because, in the middle of the night,
when I'm lonely and craving
the touch of another soul,
they at least remind me
with their moans
that in my yearning
I'm not alone.

## *Maria*
Zachary Friederich

Maria, she wasn't a ghost
She was very much alive
although she was over one thousand years old
A millennium is a long time to collect
And she filled her sets with the answers for everything asked
And she wandered from town to town
Delivering the lost the found
Oh Maria, she is the sage, she offers the truth
What you do with it, well, that part is up to you
Oh Maria, she wandered to the town of the fallen flock
To see for herself, oh, if their cause is lost
My name is Maria and I offer a light
That can pierce the shroud of clouds
that cover your town like it is of the night
You see, I've lived the years of more than ten men
And in that time I've come to find I can save the wretched
The townsfolk said you must be a witch
For anyone to live that long must surely be Godless
Oh Maria, I think she found that the curse of this town
Given the choice to sink or swim, they proudly choose to drown
Oh Maria, just one more warning about this sort
It's not the taste of meat they crave, they just kill for sport
The townsfolk said there's only one way to find the truth
We will saw her in half
and count the rings to prove her lack of youth
Oh Maria, you've got yourself into a spot
Will you get yourself out of it, I'm thinking this time probably not
Oh Maria, I'm surprised that you never surmised
That some folks will kill a spider
even though they live in a house full of flies
Oh Maria, she wasn't a ghost

## **On The Mantel**
*Daniel Medina*

On the mantel,

a glass of water and candle lay

the thirst of wandering afar,

the light of welcoming home

for those roaming to and fro netherworlds unknown

and the threshold of a home unable to release and let go.

Elysian fields were described with golden words.

Flooded are they by an abysmal sea of bitter tears,

what only longing can bring together.

Quiet, bright morns bid the phantoms adieu.

Dark nights invite shades to tarry a visit no more

as shadows pass over freeze-framed moments of long ago.

The sound of footsteps freezes my heart.

On the mantel,

an empty glass of water,

candle ghosting reminds:

never alone, always close

from golden fields afar a-watching.

### **Probate**
*Johanna Hatch*


Whose name is on the deed, the dead?
My father, which wife?
And how many certificates of marriage and death and birth and divorce
do we present to the proper authorities
before we can pay the debts?

How do we prove we are descendants of the deceased
when all we have is a name on a birth certificate?
How is that not enough?

My father left an unsigned copy of his will
and 700 dollars in a shoebox on the floor
along with 20 guns and an empty fuel oil tank.
My father left me with more questions than answers.

My father left me one-quarter of the estate.
That's 5 guns.
175 dollars.
The first floor of a haunted house
and a million things he never said.

My paperwork is in order.

*It isn't haunted, it's owned by ghosts. – Richard Siken*

## Roots Of A Haunted Past
*Kendall Hope*

I have ghosts
in the roots
of my garden.

At midnight,
the nightshades scream
in harmony
with the souls
whose bones have sunken
among layered compost
of my past hauntings.

## *Tethered*
*Mateo Leche*

I have a rope tied 'round my waist
that's tethered to my grave,
and while I can't see where it ends,
it shortens every day.

This line always extends from me
and loops all through my room,
leading me to my next steps
that fate has put in view.

I wake up and it draws me out
and down the stairs to work.
Then, when I'm done, it tows me tight
towards home in one swift jerk.

Naughty knots that do appear,
when I dare to dance off path,
they only briefly slow the tug
before untangling back.

I try to lie still like a stone
and make myself immobile,
but somehow find the less I move,
the more I'm dragged in total.

For me, it seems there is no hope
to cut or cleave this captor,
and so I'll trudge to meet my judge
and hope there's more rope after.

## The Hiding Ones
*Lachlan Woodson*

Who are they?
The other ones;
the one that hisses,
and the one that strays,

the ones in the shadows,
breaking tables in the dark,
throwing chairs out of windows.
Who are the ones that are screaming,

raging? The ones that light fires,
the ones that creep out to
set things alight
in my day-to-day time,
planting bombs
between the coffee and the rhymes.

Who are they?
The ones who cry
and cry all night,
the ones who long

for light,
who long
for peace,
yet,
fever-dreaming,
never rest.

Who are they?
Have I known them?

Once, perhaps,
when I was young
and I fell to the floor
and pounded my fists
into the carpet.

Had I met them?
Had I known them
even once?

# *The Stench of Burnt Flesh*
*Ellis Merel*

Part 1: Baptism


Heavy hands piled on their hair, still damp
from baptismal font waters. Steel teeth sparked
the elder's flint tongue, and he named it
a gift—this apparition of fire loomed behind
an eight-year-old yoked with accountability.
They called it Holy when its hands reached into
their chest, filled their stomach with summer sun
in the swell of hymns and testimony promptings.
In the dark, on the grade-school lawn, when they
felt no more than human, they felt its eyes
light solar flares to lick their spine. They halted
their thoughts, reminded themselves that this ghost
is God's Own as well. Their toys fell from the bed
and landed with their noses buried in the carpet.


Part 2: Confirmation


The oxen snorted and stomped their hooves,
faces in framed paintings curled reverent smiles
into smirks, as a twelve-year-old held their breath
on amen. A repeating prayer, an elder invoked
names they will never remember—spirits
of the deceased were branded with sainthood,
and they held the iron over the flame. Hair bound
in a cold knot, they walked down temple steps
with fire in their stomach and cattle at their heels.
In the dark, after their prayer sank into the ceiling

and spread into the walls, they struggled to sleep
to groans and stamping hooves on the floor.
Notebook pages turned, folded upon the desk.
Words they never wrote appeared within.


Part 3: Endowment


The sun unstirred from its slumber, the streets
choked on thick valley fog. The van's headlights
coughed through to guide the sixteen-year-old
and their sister to their weekday seminary,
to yawn over thin scripture pages and wince
at the scratch of chalkboard. The aging woman
called to serve as teacher read the doctrine
as written—she believed with her whole heart
every half-truth she shared. She dabbed tears
from her blush cheeks, wept over the vicious
murder of the prophet. His portrait sneered
at the room's exit, drank her cries as sacrament—
hot tar sores healed beneath his collar, feathers
contorted into hack wings. Mob-made martyr,
dragged from merciful prison and anointed
with mutant history—grotesque gilded monster
to claw doubts from buried texts, only read silent
in the dark. They stowed their answers beneath
their mattress with their confessions. The reek
of tar and simper rose from the belly of their bed.

Part 4: Sealing


A mother smiled and gave eager thanks
to her god for the company of her prodigal child,
who sat next to her in the pew. Scarlet hair and silver
jewelry marked the twenty-year-old lost livestock
in need of the crook. Saints took their hand,
welcomed them back to the flock—watched
them from a distance, raised noses to god.
Their stares, and still well-meaning kindness,
fell heavy on their stained spine. Their mother
thought their head to be bowed in prayer—
hopeful in the face of their shame. They kept
their teeth clenched firm on their apostasy.
They could not dare break their mother's heart—
confession of their departed faith ought
to deliver their corpse. Their mother's far-off
kingdom boasts iron gates, and they could never
hope to reach the steps. So quietly, softly,
in the dark, he tended to the grave of the child.
Their mother tended to the ghost of the saint.

## *Unrest*
*Lillith Era*

The closest green space to my apartment
is a cemetery.
I am told it is restful,
a quiet place to walk,
and today, in the unsettled eye of a rainstorm,
I am searching for some peace.

I am acres in, a ballroom of bones beneath my feet,
my ungrateful breath a hazy white on the December air,
when I begin to understand the heaviness that twists, wormlike,
beneath my ribcage.

There is no peace to be found here for the living.
These half-earthen bodies, these hearts lain heavy with soil,
are not unlike my own.

We both know what it is to be lost,
to understand how those we leave behind will hurt,
and still, become their ghosts.

## **Welcome To Widowhood**
*Lilith Stabs*

In the twilight's grasp, her soul does tread, her husband's voice a
memory fled.

The house lies still, a tomb of stone, where echoes linger, but she's
alone.

She guards her tears, like secrets kept, until the hour when all have
slept.

Then, in the dark, her walls unwind, but silence binds what's left
behind.

The bed, a grave of whispered dreams, awakens with the night's
extremes.

She feels him near, his breath, his weight, but knows too well her
cruel fate.

His hand, a phantom, brushes skin, a lover's touch that lies within.

Yet emptiness, it grips her tight, for he is lost to death's dark night.

The second eve, she dares to lie, again she feels his ghost draw
nigh.

A tender kiss upon her brow, but shadows speak the truth somehow.

In empty halls, where sorrow bleeds, she walks alone, where no one leads.

His presence fades, like mist at dawn, yet in her heart, he's never gone.

## *Woe's Lingering Fingers*
*Madeleine S. Cargile*

Ghosts cling to my shoulders by wispy fingers,
whispering memories that linger,
looking for pain that'll hit the ringer,
hoping I stumble and fall to their vigor.
I stop.
I hear their words, their drumming,
dropping my heart to deadened thumping.
They tut my slowed brain waves' strumming,
lamenting actions that now seem dumbing.
But I stop.
And I hold the memories close.
I accept the mistakes that created the ghosts.
I lift my hands to my woolen coat
and I pry off the hands of misery's woe.

## *Zombie*
*J. R. Marks*

You,
a ghost in the wind.
Me,
a hollowed-out shell.
A living corpse, walking a lie
amongst the feeling and the breathing.
But emotions slice and cut;
and so, I choose to omit sensation,
abandoning my beating heart
in favor of an empty cavity,
similar to your disappearance.
The severing of ties haunts my movements,
long-limbed and phantom;
I embrace the absence of feeling
in the absence of you.
Perhaps, they are one and the same,
for I could not, did not, protect my heart before;
and now, I have none left to guard.

# Living with The Shadow

## *Anger*
*Amanda Coats*

There's a mask I've worn for so long.
I put it on when I was young.
It hid me and then it became me.
And now, it's worn by default.

Pour some light into this black hole.
On a journey to save my soul.
Little girl, I'm coming back for you
because you deserve to shine.

I see you, lonely and lost in this tunnel,
with broken pieces of long-lost trouble.
You've been stuck here for so long,
unable to find your way out.

Listen to me, you've got to stay strong.
I'm learning the ropes now; hold on.
You're still here, can't you see?
Don't let go of what you want.

See, you and I, we are the same soul.
We were separated a long time ago.
This mask that became you,
take it off; it's time.

I know this life has been a struggle,
but I'm digging you out of this rubble.
You've earned your scars, but you're not gone.
Go live the life you dream about.

## **Burying The Moon**
*Jacob R. Moses*

Hollow is this daylight split
between grass and sky.

Sins are linked
between heaven and earth.

Am I rising above adversity?
Am I sinking below my standards?

Head in the ground,
tail in the air,

behind me is the rage
I simply left to burn.

Ahead of me is placidity,
leaking from my eyes.

When I ascend,
half of me will rise.

Sections of my parts
will be illuminated.

Wholeness merely exists
growing within darkness.

In the skyline of my extremity,
memories will be dichotomous.

In these burning terrains,
snakes will swallow my sorrow,

trying to bury my regret
in a plot left unmarked.

Will I be witnessed by a quorum?
Will resurrection go unnoticed?

## **Caught Between Living And Wishing To Dare**
*Caitlin Savage*

In quiet corners where the sun dips low,
a dark shadow lingers.
Muted sighs and whispered secrets,
it sways, tracing the outlines of absence.

The mirror reflects my face,
but behind me, a twisted grin glows.
She creeps along the wall,
drawing lines of fear.

Once a vibrant spirit, so full of light,
now a muted echo of a familiar face.
A cloak of my past,
a haunted testament of my memories.

Her ebon tendrils curl around my neck,
circling my fingertips.
Eyes of coal toy with my vision,
entangling my breath.

In the twilight where her whispers dwell,
she walks by my side, pulling me close.
A quiet companion, a shape that shifts,
reminding me of what I loved most.

Her edges were ripped open,
battered by time's thread.
She was pulled from my grasp,
now, a tapestry of what once was.

At times, she's heavy, an anchor of gloom,
or she'll smother me dizzy, a fog of felicity.

But in our shared dance, I've learned to walk with her.
Not as a prisoner, but as a partner.

Living with the shadows is embracing the light in loss,
to enjoy the fleeting moments.
Something shadows cannot understand—
the essence of human life.

## Doth Shadow'd In Mine Guilt's Existence
*Dr. Peter Ramos Jr.*


Murmurs whisper'd lo in breath, where no moon doth gleam,
I bide, a shade, a memory—lost in midnight's dreary'd dream.
I creep beneath yon wither'd bough, where sunlight dares not tread,
a wraith amid the hollow'd hearts, where sorrow makes its bed.

Guilt, my ceaseless torment, binds me to this pall of gray,
a chain unseen that drags me down, where light hath lost its way.
My form? A mere phantasm! A living gloom that clings,
a fleeting sigh, an echo low, where no bird ever sings.

Sorrow, like a sabl'd cloak, enshrouds me in its shade,
I choke inside its cursed folds, imprisoned in its made.
I mark my tomb from corners dark; light can never seep,
and in my hollow'd silence, drift where death doth sleeps.

The sun, like joy, in cruel neglect; hath left me in its flight,
darkness reigns as my king throned high above as shadows blight.
Now doth I live in shadows, mine guilt hath built my tomb.
In darkness, I go to liveth and grow, 'tis now my home and ruin.

A ghost within the world of men, a painful silhouette,
I linger'd longer than I dared—my hope lammed with regret.

## *Full Circle*
*Alicia Ayala (Blue Mystic)*

Upon receiving my purpose,
I was overwhelmed with emotion;

because in that very moment,
I truly understood why I had to suffer.

### *Gray // Work*
*Lindsay Valentin*


the darkness on the
sidewalk next to me
a stain I seek to scrub
away in rivers and in
creeks

let the fresh water
wash over me
as clouds slide past
above
this world curving
along free

open my eye
in the center of
my eyes
believe that I
have become something more

let in the light
when it had been
night
for what seemed
forevermore

and yet as though
I could not try
it will not go
this marking on the sidewalk
I hold

attached to me
attached to I
my darkness
is piece of my whole

## Hands Like Mine
*Jordan Nishkian*


Hands like mine
        have pink palms,
        are dark around
        knuckles and cuticles.
They are creased,
        foreseeing love,
        a happy life,
        how many babies to bear.

Hands like mine
        are soft, but not
        without callouses
        or scars from years of use.
They have raw
        patches from picked skin,
        divots from nails
        clenched too tight.

Hands like mine
        always choose "Other,"
        transitioning from white
        to brown when writing their name.
They are pretty
        (for being exotic,
        for being stained
        by spices hard to say).

Hands like mine
        claw at the whitewash,
        revealing color
        generations have buried.

They have dirt,
      caked heavy
      from the archaeology
      of culture death: of ghost-having, ghost-wanting.

## *I Should've Listened To The Shadows*
*Flor Ana*


Warmth finds itself like weight
amidst my shoulderblades.
I wish to forget,
wish to release
the relenting pain
I've put myself through.

I can't blame you,
not for all of it,
not when the shadows
had been telling me for *years*
to leave, to let go,
to let die what was already dead.

Now, I have to live with the regret,
nurture it into something
that resembles
more lesson than laceration,
because a part of me wishes to forget you *completely*,
wishes you don't haunt the halls of my hurt heart.

And I should've listened to the shadows;
should've listened before succumbing to your silence
and you became a stranger.
I should've listened to the shadows
that were begging me to see the light, to see
I always deserved better than the darkness you casted upon me.

## *Living With The Shadow*
*Damaris Chanza*

I know what it means to be the first.
The firstborn;
The first granddaughter;
The first to graduate college;
The first to deviate from the norm;
The first to disappoint.

But what if I was the second?
What if I had someone to look up to,
to lay the path,
to guide me through their mistakes?

But I'm not the second,
I'm the first.
I'm the one to look up to,
to lay the path,
to guide them through my mistakes.

Even with no one ahead of me;
No one to learn from;
I can feel their judgement.
This nonexistent older sibling,
telling me I've failed,
that I'll never get out from under their shadow;
One they never even cast.

## *Loneliness*
*Kelsey Kessler*

Loneliness is a wretched, short, twisted beast,
who makes an incision to each side of my spine,
who drinks my marrow blood with a barbed wire,
lunges into my chest,
breaks my sternum open,
digs her fingers into my wretched  heart
that morphs into a liquid rage, pooled into my stomach.
Loneliness slithers—up my throat as quick as a snake.
Crack!
Claws slide through my scalp with mindless insect intent.
Crack!
Drags my injured body only to drown me in blue water,
blue natural,
blue frigid.
A type of water that ruins my bleached hair,
soaks through my plump, blood-pooling lips.
Loneliness cusps her violent hands over my melted skin,
morphs me into any muse of her own desire.
But I think loneliness likes me the best when I am an oil painting,
but not like in a sexy Dorian Gray type of way.
But in a way where I am perfectly posed, positioned and silent,
where she can corset my rib cage,
stealing any breath of joy I have left.
Where she can hear the silence in my throat bubbling with fear.
Every time this happens,
she becomes a less-evolved creature.

In fact,
loneliness is not a monster at all.
Loneliness is a god.
Loneliness is the type of god that morphs from my armor,
to a weaponry,

to the last text I just sent to my friend,
to the sex toy hiding under my bed.
But loneliness is not the kind of god that wants to fuck you.
No.
She is the type carving me into a private Jesus,
painting a halo around my skull,
claiming I am her religion,
molding me into an entity,
claiming my body is a temple,
worshipping me like a prayer,
claiming I am cleansing her sins .
She is the type to meet my eyes,
look at me the way someone looks at a Madonna,
leaves me wanting to be drenched in her attention,
kisses the pulse beating underneath my fraudulent skin.
She hears my throat fluttering,
wanting to savor every bit of my pleasure.
My words' splinters of light that shine through her like lightening,
leaving her seethe every word I breath into a crown jewel,
wanting to trap me in an eternity of pleasure.

But I don't want loneliness to look at me
like I am Mary Magdalene.
I want to untwine the knots from my corset,
no longer having the air sucked out of my lungs.
I want to have lonliness's monstrous claws drown in a crypt,
tucking any memory of her away
as I am free.
I sometimes see her features bloom,
only to be lost in the sea of soulless faces.

### Mirror Mirror
*Elizabeth Anne Schwartz*

Women are like glass.
They break
if you hold them
too tenderly
past a respectable hour.
They bend only
for childbirth
and wedding nights;
she who looks desire
in the eye,
risks marring her reflection.
Those cracks
in her pelvis
are a warning—
she may shatter
like a brick
through stained glass,
forget that shame
should cut
like seven years of bad luck.

## *My Life Was A New Moon*
*John Queor*

My life was a new moon
with the stars shrouded
in dark storm clouds
when I heard the whispers
of a divine woman
who eventually coerced me
to step outside to cry.
And the moon was enormous.
It wrapped me up in light.
It swaddled me and held me
and made me feel alright.
The shadows were always prior
to how I felt that night.
I've descended to great depths,
but the whole time I burned bright.

## *Phobia*
*J. R. Marks*

Waves cresting and falling against the sand.
A hypnotic rhythm of sound and silence.
Above, hazy clouds and night sky listen.
The push and pull luring me in, in, in.
A wall of darkness welcomes me,
beckons me,
taunts me.
A challenge and a chase.
Seawater streams from my legs, my arms,
as I push further out, out, out.
Utter stillness beyond that thick veil.
I turn behind to see
light and shadow playing upon the water's surface,
divided as sun and moon.
But I do not turn back.
Not yet.
The darkness beyond beckons
and I reach the wall at last,
heart pounding in time to the surf upon the sand.
I stare at last into blackness
and, with a predatory grin,
It
stares back.

## **Shivers Of The Shadow River**
*Kendall Hope*

The spine of the creek
bends and twists
among horrors and mist.

The crick of my neck
tingles with sensations of fear
as I walk the path
with shadows that grasp
me by the ankles,
as if rooted like rotten trees.

And let me tell you, my dear:
there is no escape.

### The River & The Rock
*Mateo Leche*


Look down at the river
and you'll see a flowing change
as the water is new water
and the face is not the same.

Fifteen years have passed now
since you last came to this bridge
and although the wood still holds you,
you are not the same young kids.

Half your lives spent working,
after half is spent in wombs.
One more half you'll work again
just to buy your final tombs.

So when you cross this current,
keep in mind the mortal clock,
and come back to the river
with a purpose and a rock.

…then toss that stone and watch it
ripple through reflections past,
to see that change is constant.
Nothing in the water lasts.

## *The Shadow Of You*
*Vanessa 'Kaylyn Marie' Gallegos*


I live with the shadow of you,
the glimpse of your smile,
the slight smell of your scent,
the whispering sonnets
and the remains of your laughter.
I hear you in the music
and feel you in the air.
I can taste you in the smoke
and see you everywhere.

Living with the shadow of you
has led me to forgetting
that the world lost you,
finding ways you never left
as you hold me
and have my back.
You'd have to be more than a shadow to do that,
but when I think I've found you,
if I turn too fast and
the sunshine around me fills that space,
you're gone again, without a trace.

So I've gotten used to the knowing
that you're there in the shadows,
cheering me on
but reminding me not to focus on you too long;
to stay steady for what I came to do all along.

There are shadows of you
in all that I do.
My paintings reflect it,
poetry too.

The words I speak
sound like they're coming from you:
your lips,
your mouth,
your heart of steel with gold underneath,
backing my words with belief,
seeing what you meant
when you said I was captivating,
making this life worth trading
to give some of what you left with me
so the shadows aren't where you're left to be.

# *The Significance Of Spiders*
*Maverick L. Malone*


There is a lot going on right now with the energy,
with the stars, with the microcosm of me.
And though I try to convey this eloquently, inside
it is all asteroids and entomology.


There is some strange thing
that feels as if it has been missing, as if
this thing is so intricate and gossamer that it has become
the silk web of the one in which I've inevitably
become entangled without my knowing; the one


that hangs in the corner of the bedroom and quivers
when the AC kicks on; the one not all that unlike
Charlotte's except the words spelled in MINE are damn well
not the kind from bedtime stories or children's rhymes;
the one that exists to push persistence, that while I
may not be impervious to the mysterious
and often challenging lessons of this life and I shake sometimes,
there's always a rattle and roll that follows; the giddy-up
from the get-go when I let go; the one


woven across a bedroom window reeking
of a teenage dream that took me over a decade
to get close enough to believe; the one emanating
from the speakers of a carefully curated mixed CD; the one
in blood-covered bone that left me alone with only
ink and paper to soak up what was left; that web


THAT ONE
under closets and beds and blowing seemingly delicately
in breezes and breath, is anything but effortless; that web
is not a shred, and even if the spider has long since gone,

her creation remains.

Her craft contains
the brilliance and beauty of her being; the strength
of twelve hundred women that must have come before me
because *shit, my soul is old*, and it is in
the constellations superimposed on this web
that I first learned about growth, about the resilience
of the resounding human spirit, and the wonder
of waking up at all, when the light pools
and the love swells and the sky sparks. It is the web
that reminds: strength is born in the dark.

The spider is strong, but *her web*? That
is the true testament to her faith.
How much love she pours into her creations.
How much heart she weaves into every word.
How much she aches to even start in the first place.
How much space she makes to keep trying.
The will to move on from the past and engineer something
that lasts—that is never wrong.

The spider may die a thousand times,
all eight legs of hers and these eight chapters of mine,
but the light transcends; her resilience lives on.

THIS LIFE is the one
she finds where she BELONGS.

## Tonight The Dead Will Feast
*H. R. Parker*


They planted my body
in a graveyard
(like a budding flower).
But I ripped
up
my
roots.
I will not stay buried.
Vengeance
has set my soul aflame.

Your soul
called to me,
a beacon
in a raging tempest,
a blinking lighthouse
on a distant shore.
The smell of vengeance
hung in the air,
but I couldn't taste it
(just yet).

Your screams
as I hovered
in your dark corners
(an aperitif),
so delectable;
the main course:
setting your mind
alight
(night after night)
with the horror

of my last moments on earth.

I dragged your body
still flickering
with the flame of life.
I tucked you away
(in my tomb).

Now:
I eat your body
(snack on your soul)
while you cleave
to the small flame of life
I allow you to have.

Your eternal suffering
(my dessert);
how delicious.

## The Red Fox Fur Coat
Carmen Misé

I used to hang there in the furrier's old shop by the window, day in and day out, collecting dust, waiting. Before that, I couldn't tell you. My memory is shaped like pieces of broken glass, never quite put back together the same way, never whole, forever distorted. Now, I can only recount my days in the furrier's shop, when I was taken out of a box, shaken, brushed, fluffed, and placed on the mannequin. The others who lived in my home were not like me. I was special, unique, spellbinding. My red hue shone vividly, like blood from a cut. There, by the window, I saw life pass by. Each morning and every sunset, rain or shine, snow or hail. Men on their way to work, children on their way to school, women about their business, but I was unimpressed.

After a while, I became accustomed to my home, on the mannequin, by the window, in the furrier's shop, until one day I saw her. I noticed her before she noticed me, as she walked home from her job at the bank. And it was on one of those days that she first laid eyes on me, there on the mannequin, by the window, in the furrier's old shop. She stopped and I could see her shiver, fidget, and that look of desire. I desired her too. Her body against my skin, together, close, warm. The store was closed for the night, but I knew she would be back the following day, and she did. That night I thought of her, lying in bed, thinking of me. She came in the next day, flustered, in a hurry, distressed. I heard her inquire over me to the saleswoman. They spoke in hushed tones to each other, and she seemed to relax. I had not been sold. "It could have been made for you," said the saleswoman as she put me on and looked at herself in the mirror. "I was," I whispered to her, "made for you."

*Inspired by Teolinda Gersao's short story, "The Red Fox Fur Coat"*

## *Walking Silhouettes*
*Claire Kroening*

Shadows mend the crooked floorboards while the city sleeps.
Tracing absent lines of devils in disguise,
forced to live in a constant
nine to five,
we let the moments die
before grasping a chance to see
in more than merely black and white.
Shadows mend the crooked floorboards;
always there, always watching,
until we succumb
to walking silhouettes
in our dreams.

# WITCH'S
# BREW

## *A Whisper Of Bloods And Tears*
*H. R. Parker*

Butterflies love
the taste of blood.
Did you know that?
I lay on the ground,
the blood
of my latest repast
dripping from my mouth.
A magnificent feast.

The butterflies agreed.
So did their night cousins
(the moths).

I lay there
unmoving,
a fat tick upon a dog's back
filled to the brim
(with the blood of innocents).
The bodies lay
s c a t t e r e d about me;
deflated skins
like discarded balloons
after a child's birthday party.

Then, they came:
the butterflies.
Later, the moths.
Tickling my mouth
with their ever-searching proboscis,
probing
for the dead sighs
that lingered upon my lips

sealed shut with congealed blood
and the pilfered dreams
of the dead.

Now these creatures
follow me
(wherever I go)
whispering of blood and tears.

## *And Is That Not Love? Part II*
*Lillith Era*

Around my neck,
in a heart-shaped locket,
I keep
the soft curl of her hair,
& the wink she gave with it.

On her altar,
surrounded by a collection of forget-me-nots,
she keeps
a candle, pomegranate red,
poured gentle, hot wax dripping onto nimble hands,

As if this isn't spell work,
little love potions slipped into warm drinks of nonchalant.

Come, share a cup with me—
Burt's Bees saccharine on ceramic mouth
an incantation for a kiss, wordless and still.

I like to tell you that you make me nervous.
You don't.
You warm me up,
Like a hot drink on a cold day,
you alchemize me,
until I am radiant throughout.

# How To Bake Him Your Boyfriend, Brujita
*Annie Vazquez*

On Venus day, aka Fridays, or *viernes*,
witches, or brujitas, around the world cast love spells and
create clandestine bindings.
The moon, or *la luna*, and their familiars are the only ones
privy to witness.

Shhhh

If you can keep a secret, or a *secreto*,
I will share such sorcery with you.
But you are forewarned:
you will get exactly what you concoct before
the next 2 Full Moons, or *Lunas Illena*, rise.
Make sure his heart, or *corazon*, drums pure love,
he belongs to no one else and he bears no ill karma
as you inherit him all:
Demon or Angel.
Now, *brujita*, if you are ready,
get 1 red candle, or *velita roja*,
state your petition for him and light it.
This recipe must be complete, or *completada*,
before the candle melts like glaze on top of a donut.

Inside a giant pot, or *cazeula*, deposit the following:
1 stick of his deep delicious buttery laugh,
half a cup of his milk, dark or white chocolate hair
(if his hair is red, or *rojo*, substitute for cinnamon),
sprinkle 2 salty tears, or *lagrimas*, from his mesmerizing eyes,
3 tablespoons of his sugary, or sweet as *azucar*, kisses,
1 cup of flour, or *harina*,
1 cup of milk, or *leche*,
and lastly, the most important ingredient: 1 teaspoon of vanilla.

Vanilla is the elixir of the goddess of love,
bringing aphrodisiac qualities.
Mix together, envisioning him as already yours.
Now, *brujita*, bake in the oven at 375 ° for 12 minutes and 12 seconds
(the angel number to call in love and remove blocks).
Let cool and then eat with a tall glass of milk while
making a list of beautiful qualities he will come with.

### How To Bring A Dead Thing Back To Life
*Maverick L. Malone*


You were there to live a twilight flicker until you learned
you were forest fire. All night, waging war against yourself,
gone too far, allowing the all-consuming
to consume you, but it wasn't the all-consuming
you were meant to be.

Ageless wisdom churned your knowing,
burned the bark from the branch. Left a hole
like a hull and there you made a home.
Charred archways you accepted
from anyone who came calling to your threshold,
too soon abandoning your birthright.

You were famine, blight. Don't pay
the high price of their advice. You
are not here to tread lightly.
You do not fear the night.
You are redwood tall and born in flame—
you are the one you seek to find.

## *Jigunda Losses Of The Night Before*
*Jen Kropinak*


Opamp lifts her soiled head. Now neck, now toes.
She is both above and below, hitting rock bottom.

90 days past due, the broken screen door, cut knees on
the hinges, falling into a familiar rhythm, always hungry,
dead mice in the pantry. She remembers him trying to slip
through the underside of her door. Cattywompus hurricanes,
mixed with whiskeyknives leaving a ring around the rosie.

But she held hemlock to his face, cursed him to another
place, never finding the body. After that, in her kreened a nuance
of fierce responsibility, as she was shown the secret places
and streams, had to shed skin seven times over to unleash
the forgotten meaning. Now a protector of children and the
lost, she waits for no one, for she knows what life costs.

Now Opamp hocks up a good one and laughs.
Gathers the day, cracks open a Pabst.

And sure, she mourns… whaddyagittinat? Because early in the
morning, when the TV is low—the transient voltage suppressor in
her chest runs lower still, allowing her to sip from 10 lives or 20.

Opamp purses her lips, lights up a smoke,
calls him at 3 a.m. and talks to his ghost.

# Lilith

*Elizabeth Anne Schwartz*

They never speak
of Adam's first wife—
who fled the garden
of her own accord,
refused to answer
to mankind,
sprouted horns
and bat wings
and frightened
obedient wives
with black eyes
and forked tongue.
She became
her own mistress,
a legend
men don't dare voice.

## *Magick*
*Daniel Medina*

In this age, beguiled by want,

such a culture of death,

magick slips through the crowds,

safeguarded by masters accustomed to the light.

Yarrow as poultice for scars, pain, and suffering

the spells of healing.

Some stir, some recite.

Still, others ask the sky

to love, to heal, to be closer to the divine.

Some read leaves, others, the stars. Still, others use herbs, bark, and root.

A sorcerer's brew said to be abominable.

A sorcerer's brew said to be magical.

A sorcerer's brew said to be true,

crossing the street when you should've walked further,

bumping into him when it should've been her.

We've all encountered magick.

We've all been to a few

who saw beyond our limits and saw what was true.

## *Rituals*
*Cristina Menendez*


Place salt on hands and scrub out the old.
Wash hands in water to cleanse and call in the new.
With this ritual,
I am clean;
light a candle and pray
that the light comes through me and from me.
With this ritual,
I am bright;
ignite smoke and set the intention to cleanse the energy in me and
around me.
With this ritual,
I am truth;
call to a lover, adorn with passionate kisses
the sacred orgasm.
With this ritual,
I am free;
lay hands on body,
taking deep breaths.
With this ritual,
I am present;
play favorite music
and begin to dance.
With this ritual,
I am releasing;
stand outside and hug
a tree.
With this ritual,
I am grounded in nature's healing;
sit by the ocean and smell the salty breeze.
With this ritual,
I am peaceful.

## Salamander Stew

*Kendall Hope*

Witch's brew,
salamander stew.
Silken white hair
hangs over the caldron
as children stare,
awaiting their fate.
A potion with
plenty to share,
do not let it waste.
Now have a taste.

## Sleep Potion
*John Queor*


Bubbling away goes the kettle
as all my problems stay inside,
a little bit ignored and solidified
like instant oatmeal caked on the lip
of the bowl left in the sink after breakfast.

Chamomile, lavender, lemongrass,
catnip, valerian, mugwort, and peppermint.

Steeped for at least five minutes
to untie the knots in your stomach
and remind you what it felt like
to fall asleep while watching cartoons
as perhaps you did like me as a kid.

Peppermint, mugwort, valerian, catnip,
lemongrass, lavender, and chamomile.

Steeped for at least five minutes
with a dash of honey for sweeter dreams
or some kava kava for lucidity.

If you decide to try this recipe,
do not use heavy machinery.

## *The Brujas In The Sala*
*Damaris Chanza*

The ingredients are simple,
an old family recipe,
passed on from *tía* to *tía*,
for generations of *Latinas*,
over a little *cafecito* in the *sala*.
They learned it from their *abuelas*.

The measurements vary;
The ancestors tell them what's perfect,
the *cafecito* just an accessory,
an excuse to gather,
to prolong the goodbye.

The real recipe lies in the scene.
The *tías, hermanas, mamis, hijas, abuelas,* and *nietas,*
all the *nenas* sitting in the *sala*,
on floral *sofás* covered in plastic,
laughing, cackling,
relaying the latest *chisme*;
instilling superstitions;
*El Mal De Ojo,*
*La Curandera;*
*Brujerias.*

Still, there's a secret ingredient;
One that bonds these *brujas*;
A magic that cannot be undone.
The secret ingredient;
Love.

## The Sacrifice
*Alicia Ayala (Blue Mystic)*

If pain is beauty,
if pain is art,
then I am a masterpiece.

My self-destruction
is my creation.

## **The Witch And Her Red-Eyed Imp**
*Lilith Stabs*

In the heart of the woods where the shadows weep, there lives a witch in her lair so deep.
Her eyes like coals, her heart a tomb, wrapped in whispers, and cloaked in gloom.

By her side, in the pale moon's gleam, hops a creature like a ghost in a dream.
A little white bunny with eyes blood-red, silent as sorrow, a thing of dread.

They wander the night through mist and pine. Two cursed souls on a path serpentine.
The witch, with her spells, weaves fate anew, and the bunny, her familiar, watches it brew.

In shadows they dance; in darkness, they play, bound by a curse that won't decay.
The witch and her bunny, a bond so tight, in a world where day surrenders to night.

And when the winds wail and the owls take flight, the witch whispers secrets to the dead of night.
Her bunny listens, eyes aglow, n the haunted woods where no one dares go.

For they are the keepers of sorrow and dread, the witch and her bunny, the living and the dead. A tale untold, a secret kept, n the heart of the woods where the shadows wept.

## **Un-Love Potion**
*Ashley Lilly*

Fresh rainwater
to cleanse my mind of you.
Chamomile with mustard yellow pistils
to calm the storm in my beating heart.

Fresh-picked blueberries
for protection,
and to help me speak
my mind.

A few sweet drizzles
of lavender syrup
to attract what is calm
and tranquil.

A squeeze of lemon
to make this resolution last;
infused with black obsidian
to be set free from toxicity.

### *Untitled*
*Birdy Wolfe*

I am concerning
and I am intense.
I kiss god on the mouth
and masquerade my sins.

I speak eloquently
of tragedy and purgatory,
but goddamn it, I'm lucky
to have a tongue
still a part of me.

I smoke tobacco,
thinly rolled into
circle-shaped fantasies,
and my pack is orange.
It'll forever remind me
of my friend's eternal memories.

I pray to the saints
that they're still watching
because I'm an orchid
blooming, growing casually.

I can't erase my fantasies.
I can't undo the ecstasy.
I can't undo the afternoons
that I spent not a part of me.

That self feels so distant to me;
I no longer belong to agony.

My pain is not nostalgic

because I will find myself
in Antigone
and Heracles,
and every stone thrown
from a man no more mortal
than my favorite tree.

I am bridging the gap
between the natural world
and fantasy; it is my belief
that this earth is a part of me,
that I may be a dancing wind,
that I am the rushing spirit of a flood,
that I'm the filtering silt of
everything
that's come before me.

And most importantly,
I am not the confines of my body
because my *I*
finally belongs to my
me.

## **Nightmare #925**
*Gabriela Lauren De La Torre*


Life is so cruel to the
lame and barren woman
dreaming of a life
where she can stand
beneath the moonlight
and watch the bodies of her
ex-boyfriend and his new lady
swing back and forth—
holding a knife
in her hands.

## Vengeance
*Caitlin Savage*

The blood of all those you burned
runs slick in our veins.

Trees moan and the wind screams,
howls of our ancestors still strong.

The hunters thought they ended our reign,
but our magic cannot be tamed.

The green glow of the cauldron
ignites flames in our eyes.

Just like the bodies of the men,
who named our power as evil.

Spells dance on our lips,
hands sway with the guild of our voices.

Cackles mock the tranquil night air,
our figures circle the spire of smoke.

Their screams of fear excite us
as our plan for revenge unfolds.

## Witch's Brew
*Vanessa 'Kaylyn Marie' Gallegos*

To be like you,
inviting and sweet,
friendly to all that I meet,
a loving mom,
a strong friend,
someone who's got your back times 10,
who will remind you,
time and time again,
how to rebuild by lending a hand.
I'd stir in,
the depression and confusion too,
because I need to truly feel like you:
a connection to others only an empath like you could get.
A dash of sass
and lots of love to go with it,
kneading it like masa before the *tortillas* begin
and making sure to throw all the silliness in,
to be able to laugh at myself with friends.
I would add in some comfort
that you can only get from your hug
and I'd throw in some medicine
that only your love can provide.
A witch's brew, to be like you.
To bottle you up
and savor every bit,
for when by your side I won't be able to sit.
There has to be some thoughtfulness
mixed in with the playfulness
and a tender heart to separate it with.
There's also stubbornness,
some people-pleasing tendencies thrown in.
But once we get it all fin,

it will be sealed with magic,
for the *bruja* who started us,
these *brujitas* will never turn to dust,
for we will never forget the strength
that this foundation was built upon.
And even in darkness, we will push on.
We will create the life we lust
to do that.
Honor this witch, we must.

## Witch's Prayer
*Eyajo December Joseph*

The earth unfolds its veils tonight,
this haunting Hollow's eve.
Witches gather your tools, but
let no one see! The elementals
speak tonight for all the worlds
to hear. They're chanting hymns of love
and indescribable fear.

Faeries ride fallen leaves
in a whirlwind to our world.
Kings, queens, lords, and ladies
from lands faraway west.
They've come to hire witches,
the ones that spell the best!

Crenunnos and Dana have come
to greet us all. They bring gifts of
magic to their children
and tales of giants tall!
Blood drips down, drop by drop,
from oak trees of the priests.
Collected in silver goblets
and offered to the demon priests.
Heroes from the other worlds
have come to find that witch,
that cunning  creature whose
soul always shape-shifts.

Meanwhile, on a hilltop, a
fire is burning blue. There's a
black cauldron invoked with
some strange witch's brew.

Children play on burial grounds
and pose with vampire teeth.
They play these malice games
to scare the twilight thief.

Now, lay me down to begin
the witch's prayer.
I'm sure the otherworld will
listen. I'm sure they'll judge
fair!

Faeries ride fallen leaves
in a whirlwind to our world.
Kings, queens, lords, and ladies
from lands faraway west.
They've come to hire witches,
the ones that spell the best!

Now, I'm not going to tell you
the witches that get to go.
The ones who pray understand.
They're the ones who know.

# THE POETS

***Flor Ana*** is a Cuban-American writer, singer, and poet who loves to make people feel something through her words. She is the author of a handful of poetry collections, and her debut novel, Amanita, was released in October 2024. She is also an event poet on occasion with her typewriter. When Flor is not writing, she is helping other writers through Indie Earth Publishing, singing or creating musical compositions to accompany her poetry, and exploring nature. // ***@littleearthflower***

***Aphrodite's Devotee (Paiige)*** is a poet, intuitive tarot reader, and Reiki Master from Florida. She has been writing poetry since she was 15, and with her spiritual journey, her work has evolved into a collection of poems meant to tap into the soul's inner dialogue. She believes that poetry and the creative arts in general are capable of healing people deeply. She has been featured in various anthologies, including *Glow: Self-Care Poetry for the Soul* and *The Spell Jar: Book of Shadows*.
***@venusastria***

***Ash Autumn*** is a musician, writer, and environmental researcher currently based in Austin, Texas. As a child in small-town Wisconsin, she received local accolades after competing in short story competitions. She held her first live story reading at age 9! Now she's on a journey to explore her place within the world of creative writing as an adult.
***@ash_autumn_stateofheart***

***Sam Avocado*** is a Colorado native who transplanted to the Emerald Coast of Florida. He is a published author for his work in the study of microbes ranging from bacteriophages to sourdough starter bacterial communities. Nowadays, he finds himself reconnecting with his favorite hobbies of gardening, spending time in nature, and writing. Being a first-generation Mexican-American, it helps him feel grounded in both cultures to be able to express himself creatively in both English and Spanish. // *@samavocado*

***Alicia Ayala (Blue Mystic)*** is a singer, songwriter, poet, and multidimensional artist from Miami, Florida. Her music and poetry showcase a natural ability to connect with universal flow to channel emotion, soul experiences, and spiritual wisdom. Transmuting darkness into light and expanding consciousness is the driving force behind her craft. She aims to comfort and inspire others on their healing journey as they collectively strive for self-mastery. With her otherworldly, cosmic essence and thought-provoking quotes, she dives deep into the streams of consciousness of her audience. // *@_bluemystic*

***Madeleine S. Cargile*** currently attends Auburn University in pursuit of a Bachelor's in Speech, Language, and Hearing Sciences. She's had over a dozen pieces of poetry and short stories published in various literary magazines and anthologies. Along with reading and writing, she enjoys art, embroidery, and jamming out to heavy metal music. // *@madeleinescargilewrites*

***Jessi Carman*** is a lifelong storyteller dedicated to finding what feels solid in the void. She writes poetry, prose, and nonfiction and is least protective of her poetry. They love books, film, crystals, their cats, and all strange things. // *@jessimoons*

***Damaris Chanza*** is a poet and copywriter from Orange, New Jersey. Her work has appeared in the New Jersey Bards Poetry Review 2024 and NJArts.net. She has a Bachelor's in Communication and Media from NJIT and runs Discussions with Damaris, a blog about representation and diversity in media. Damaris enjoys playing with her ferret and collecting Snow White memorabilia. To learn more about Damaris visit Damarischanza.com. // ***@damarischanza***

***Amanda Coats*** is a southern small-town girl with a multifaceted yet soft-spoken heart. She's a committed wife, mother, and lover of all things nature. She's a hairstylist, writer, and yogi. Essentially, she is a student of self, life, and love, determined to bloom in the darkness on her path to presence, peace, and contentment. She lives in Northwest Florida with her family and four-legged friends. Her hobbies include yoga, reading, baking, and spending time outdoors. You may remember her from The Spell Jar: Book of Shadows. Be on the lookout for her debut poetry collection. // ***@poet.treebyac***

***Gabriela Lauren De La Torre*** is a poet based in Las Vegas, Nevada. Originally a formal student of the sciences, she decided after many years of intense academic study to follow her creative passions and pursue a literary career. Now she writes and publishes regularly in English, Spanish, and Portuguese, drawing inspiration from her dreams, romance, and her life as a classical violinist studying physics at university. And of course, her poetry would not be where it is today if were not for all the cringey men and women of the world who so generously provide much of the material for her writing :) // ***@gab.aah***

***Michael Deman*** is an acrylic painter, poet and prose writer, born and raised in Jersey City, New Jersey. As a volunteer across many avenues, he aims to feed love through art into as many people as possible. With a background in radio and film, Michael loves staying creative and inspiring others to do the same. // ***@geographicalgravy***

***Lilith Era*** is a poet, actor, & singer based in Oakland, California. When not writing or performing, she can be found planning arts & cultural events at her day job, cooking meals with love, or sending sappy text messages to her beloved friends & partner. // ***@Lillithera***

***Jacquelynne Faith*** is a lifelong writer, having written her first book, *Mi Trip 2 New Yorc,* before she could even spell. Now, she spells in many ways with a background in professional copy-writing and editing, a degree in Human Communication from UCF, and a career as an oracle and priestess (for real!). You can also find her stepping into her magic in the form of witches, sirens, and mermaids as a professional model and credited actress. // ***Instagram: @jacquelynnefaith***

***Zachary Friederich*** is a songwriter and poet from New York. His songs have been featured in many films and television shows and his poetry has been published in numerous literary magazines. // ***@zacharyfriederich***

***Vincent J. Hall II*** is a New Jersey-based writer who made his literary debut with The Drinks Between Us. A History graduate from William Paterson University, Vincent helps lead ArtPride New Jersey Foundation's advocacy and governmental affairs efforts. When he is not helping his community and advocating for arts and culture, Vincent enjoys attending Phillies games with his partner Megan, going to museums, and spending time with friends. // *@vincevangoah*

***Johanna Hatch*** is a poet writing at the intersection of nature, kinship, and magic. A native of Cape Cod, Massachusetts, she now lives in Wisconsin with her family. Her poetry has also been featured in *The Spell Jar: Poetry for the Modern Witch, Glow: Self-Care Poetry for the Soul,* and *Grieving as Shapeshifting: Spells for Coming Undone.* // *@johannajanet*

***Kendall Hope*** is a Colorado native, who thrives off of sunshine and creativity. She loves exploring the outdoors and being a part of nature, which translates into her poetry. She is the author of Pockets of Lavender and The Willow Weepings, which won a Gold Literary Titan Award in 2023. Kendall also recently published her junior poetry collection, Tongue Tied, and her works can be found in local stores in Colorado Springs, like Poor Richard's, Ivywild School, and Barnes & Noble Briargate. *@kendallhopepoetry*

***Eyajo December Joseph*** is a poet of the surreal, dark and un-canny. His style varies from lyrical, narrative, satirical, confes-sional and fairytale-esque (leaning toward the darker side of twisted romantic tragedies and mournful Dirges). He is also the vocalist/lyricist/chief-songwriter of the goth rock/deathrock band Black Heroin Gallery and was the co-founder, chief-lyri-cist/keyboardist/co-songwriter of the legendary deathrock band Astrovamps, as well as a surrealist painter and illustrator. His poetry and art have been published in a handful of underground magazines and his lyrics have been recorded on a number of underground albums. He lives in Los Angeles, California. *@e.december_joseph*

***Vanessa 'Kaylyn Marie' Gallegos*** resides in Denver, Colorado with her family, is on the cusp of her thirties and spends her time making art, doing runway shows, and acting. Poetry has always been a way to express her feelings and life experiences and she utilizes this to connect with those who are unable to put their own feelings into words. Find Kaylyn Marie in nine other anthologies curated by Shannon O'Connor, R. Clift, Indie Earth Publishing, PoetsChoice, and Jack Wild Publishing. *@art_by.ness*

***Kelsey Kessler*** is a writer based in Boston, Massachusetts. She recently performed in the 2024 VoxPop regional poetry slam festival and the 2024 NorthBeast regional poetry slam festival. She was also featured on the Viewless Wings podcast. Although she is most known for writing horror poems, she explores top-ics of queer identity and mental health. Kelsey also works as a clinical social worker. *@witchinghourss*

***Claire Kroening*** is a writer of picturesque poetry and prose based in the upper Midwest region of the United States. Their work has been published in a multitude of online and print magazines worldwide, including *The Greyhound Journal*, *Thoughts Hymn Publishers*, and *Vellichor Literary Magazine*, among others. When not working on their latest endeavors, they appreciate visiting art museums and studying creative writing. *@clairerosek*

***Jen Kropinak*** is a mother, writer, and artist from Pittsburgh, Pennsylvania. She earned her BA in English and MA in Journalism & Mass Communication. Jen's literary work has appeared, or is forthcoming, in *Generation Magazine, Dionne's Project, The Rebis, MEMEZINE*, and *Ouch! Collective*. She was recognized as a poetry semifinalist in the 2024 Patty Friedmann Writing Competition. // *@momumonsterzine*

***Mateo Leche*** loves you very much, and every poem he writes is for you, the animals, the plants, the planets, the stars, and the universe that holds us. // *@el.matt.adore*

***Hannah Levy*** is a writer, poet, and founder of The Rebis, an annual tarot literary anthology. In her past lives, she led content marketing and brand strategy for tech companies and served as editor-in-chief of the music blog Indie Shuffle. In her free time, she's horseback riding, walking through the redwoods, stargazing, reading erotic poetry, and playing extensive make-believe games with her daughter. *// @hnnhlvy*

***Ashley Lilly*** is a queer, African American poet from New York. Their writing has been featured in *The Spell Jar: Book of Shadows, Glow: Self-Care Poetry For The Soul, Footnotes by The Poetry Project*, the *Black Poppy Review*, and the *Inspirations Anthology*. Ashley has self-published several poetry books including *Wanderer* and *Young Heart*, as well as a collection of short stories titled *Impossible Things*. Ashley holds a Bachelor of Arts in English from LIU Post. *// @ashleyscribblesink*

***Maverick L. Malone*** is an author, editor and spoken word artist who believes wholeheartedly in the magic and healing power of words. Maverick published her first poetry book, *Pressed Petals*, in 2022 with her second, *Hope and Other Beautiful Things* in spring of 2024. Maverick's third book will shock everyone and will be released sometime in 2025. In addition to writing, she also hosts the podcast Ink Speak and co-leads hiking and writing retreats through the women-centric community, Superbloom Society. *// @mavmalone @superbloomsociety*

***J. R. Marks*** is a poetess whose work explores themes of mental health, trauma recovery, and romance in modern society. A single mother living in the Alabama countryside, she balances her days as a healthcare worker and her nights as a writer while desperately chasing the illusive dream of one day living alone in the woods as the local hag. Her poetry has been featured in multiple anthologies, and she is currently working on a collection that delves into each of these topics. Jordan looks forward to the release of her debut poetry collection, *Love in the Time of Corona*, in 2025. *// @jordan.r.marks.poetry*

***Heather Meatherall*** is a poet and writer from Canada. Her work has been published in magazines such as *The Icarus Writing Collective* and *Mythos Magazine*, and she was a featured writer in the *Dreams in Hiding* anthology. When she isn't writing she can be found coding, crocheting, or throwing her DND characters into new and exciting situations. // *@heathermeatspoetry*

***Daniel Medina*** was born in Chicago, Illinois, and raised in Miami, Florida. A graduate of Florida International University, he went on to serve in U.S. Military Intelligence. He holds graduate degrees from the University of Oklahoma and St. Thomas University (Florida Center for Theological Studies), Miami Gardens, FL, where he earned his doctorate with distinction. Daniel has also written and presented lectures on several topics, including Charles Williams' Theology of Romantic Love and Co-Inherence, Zen Meditation, Mindfulness, World Religions and Spirituality, Conflict Resolution, José Marti, and the American Transcendentalist Movement. Dr. Medina is a public schoolteacher and an ordained minister with the United Church of Christ. He is also a painter, musician, photographer, and the author of *KIGO: Four Seasons in Haiku.* // *@baxtermonkink*

***Angelica Medlin*** is a part-time lecturer of English composition at California State University of Fullerton in sunny Southern California. She lives there with her mother, her partner, and one very sassy dog. She has worked in academia for a decade as a writing tutor and educator, as well as for CSUF's DASH literary journal. Angelica is currently completing her first novel in the fantasy genre as she continues writing poetry about everything from monsters to the power of friendship. // *@thebrujapoeta*

***Cristina Menendez*** is an artist whose purpose is to create by being inspired. She studied theatre and motion picture business at the University of Miami, then pivoted into marketing and event planning, working for brands like MTV, Sony LATAM, Disney, Saks Fifth Avenue and Burberry. Her next transition was motherhood and organically learning about emotional intelligence, which led to her becoming a Reiki Master, Medical Intuitive, Light Language channeler and Sound bowl player. Recently, Cristina has had featured poems in Love Letters to the 305, and regularly writes inspiring soul-led words, which she shares with the community. Cristina now offers to guide those called to their own purpose through Energetic Activations, casting magic on the shadows so we can love them. // *@cristyhappyplace*

***Ellis Merel*** is a queer writer and artist originally from the Central Valley of California. Ever since they discovered the spoken word poetry scene in high school circa 2013, they've been in love with performance ever since. In addition to their love for writing fiction and prose, they've been known to draw every once in a while. // *@ellis.merel*

***Carmen Misé*** is an Assistant Professor of Composition and Literature at Miami Dade College. The Miami-Dade Public Library System invited Carmen to launch their Art and Sculpture Lecture Series, where she delivered a lecture on national identity, memory, and Counter-Monuments—a theory she explored in her master's thesis and continues to examine in her writings. Her most recent non-fiction work, *Inherited Trauma and Memories That Are Not Our Own*, was published in *Luna Luna*, an online magazine. Carmen's latest poetry includes *Realization* in Sonder Magazine, a journal of cultural criticism and creative writing, *When Mangos Last in My Backyard Bloom'd* in Waterproof: Evidence of a Miami Worth Remembering, and *Ode to the Guava Pastelitos* in the zine Miami Grubs: Meals and Memories. Her debut children's book, *A Cat Almost Stole Mom's Car*, was published in the Summer of 2024.
***@carmen_mise_***

***Jacob R. Moses*** is a poet and spoken word artist from Staten Island, NY. Publications featuring his work span the globe. He is the author of the full-length poetry book, *Grimoire*, and is currently a graduate student at Southern New Hampshire University, pursuing a Masters in English and Creative Writing. Each poem in this anthology was an assignment.
***@jacobreubenmoses***

***Jordan Nishkian*** is an Armenian-Portuguese writer based in California. Her prose and poetry explore themes of duality and have been featured in national and international publications. She has been awarded the Rollick Magazine Fiction Prize and has received nominations for the Pushcart Prize and Best American Short Stories. Jordan is the Editor-in-Chief of *Mythos* literary magazine and the author of *Kindred*, a novella.
***@wordsbyjordan***

***John Queor*** is an equinox, existing equally in the dark and light. He lives in a tower in Central New York, and spends quite a bit of his time writing poetry in the light of the moon. John has two poetry collections out, *Burnt Lavender* and *Resembling A Moth*, with a third being published in 2024. John has been included in three anthologies, and recently was published in a local history magazine. // *@johnnyqu33r*

***H.R. Parker*** is an author, poet, and editor who hails from the subtropical wilds of Georgia. She has had over one hundred poems and short stories featured in numerous literary magazines and online publications, such as *Clover & Bee Magazine, Nightingale & Sparrow, Ghostwatch Paranormal Zine*, and *Fairfield Scribes*. When she's not reading or writing, she's haunting graveyards, cuddling cute, furry animals, or embracing her hobbit DNA and eating po-tay-toes. // *@authorhrparker*

***Dr. Peter J. Ramos Jr.*** lives in Southern California. He is an author, digital artist, and Doctor of World Religious Studies. He is the creative director and founder of Hous of Ibiko. He has written books such as *Hello Enzo: What Does Enzo Like To Do?* and *Happy In A Thousand Dark Places*. His latest book, *And Then I Woke Up, Screaming*, is his first collection of short stories. // *@hous.of.ibiko*

***Ila S.*** is a teenage writer, poet, lyricist, and musician who believes that words really can make a difference. Her goal is that her writing changes or heals at least one heart, and to show that life doesn't have to be a burden. She does her best to use her voice to advocate for mental health, against racism, and more. *@ila.writes7*

*Caitlin Savage* was born and raised in Miami—loving the city, but longing for mountains. Caitlin considers her family and friends as the most important part of her life. If not writing poetry, you will find her baking cookies on rainy days or her nose buried deep in a horror novel. // *@caitlin.skyee*

*Cassandra Alexandra Soldo* is a senior at Agnes Scott College, pursuing her Bachelor's degree in Creative Writing with minors in Psychology and Film Studies. Born and raised in New Jersey, she brings an assertive voice to her work. Cassandra has a fascination with ghosts, exploring their role as remnants or echoes in her featured poem, *Ghostly Hymns*. Her poetic debut was in the first volume of *The Spell Jar,* and she is excited to return for the third volume. // *@cassandra_soldo*

*Lilith Stabs* is known for acting in indie horror movies and modeling in pinup magazines and comic books. She loves working both sides of the camera. She is an artist who works mostly with acrylics and mixed-media collages. She is also an EDM musician, but writing is her big passion, as well as bunnies. Lilith Stabs has two rescue rabbits she resides with in Redondo Beach, California. // *@vampybunny*

*Elizabeth Anne Schwartz* writes sapphic fiction and poetry, and loves all things dark, lyrical, and confessional. She earned her BA in Creative Writing at Purchase College. Her chapbook, *Nine Stages of Coming Out*, was released by tiny wren lit. *@elizanneschwa*

***Lindsay Valentin*** is a writer and creative artist living in Los Angeles, California. She has written poetry, fiction, and non-fiction on travel, culture, lightwork, and lesbian life in print and online for GO NYC Magazine, BUST Magazine, Defy Magazine, Pink Pangea, Indie Earth, White Stag Press and Querencia Press. She works deeply with herbs and reiki and is a part of the West Coast mystic and sound healing communities.
***@lvalentin77***

***Annie Vazquez*** is a Pug Mom to Elmo and Petunia. She is a poet, writer and former journalist, featured in the Miami Herald, Refinery29, NBC6 and Good Morning America. Annie is known for pioneering fashion blogging in Miami and is also the gal behind Annie The Alchemist, a site dedicated to teaching people how to meditate and manifest. She is the author behind *My Little Prayer Book: 75 Prayers, Poems & Mantras for Illumination* and the upcoming *My Little Spiritual Book: Rituals, Poems & Practices for Enlightenment.* // ***@anniethealchemist***

***Lachlan Woodson*** is a queer poet and indie journalist from the backwoods of the Florida Panhandle. The friction of being queer in a place that oppresses them inspires their most powerful poems. Lachlan is a street poet that serves their community and makes a living by writing personal poems for everyday folks right on the sidewalk. They enjoy living in an 80 year old cottage in the woods with their two queer-Shakespeare-named cats, Imogen and Rosalind. // ***@lachlanwoodson***

# INDIE EARTH

PUBLISHING

## *About The Publisher*

Indie Earth Publishing is an author-first, independent publishing company based in Miami, FL, dedicated to giving artists and writers the creative freedom they deserve in publishing their poetry, fiction, and short stories. We provide our authors a plethora of services that are meant to make them feel like they are finally releasing the book of their dreams, including professional editing, design, formatting, organization, advanced reader teams, and so much more. With Indie Earth Publishing, you're more than just another author, you're part of the Indie Earth creative family, making a difference in the world, one book at a time.

www.indieearthbooks.com

For inquiries, please email:
indieearthpublishinghouse@gmail.com

Instagram: @indieearthbooks